Book Desc

Does your kid always run to their room when scolded, throws a tantrum in the middle of the road, uses abusive language, and misbehaves with their peers and elders? Or do they seem scared to take on new challenges because the fear of failure and loss is too much to handle? Are they not mentally strong to regulate their emotions and behaviors? Do they show reluctance to try things they aren't comfortable with? Are you afraid the outside world will break their confidence and manipulate them?

If so, then this is the book you need to read right now!

Often kids, young and old, fear trying new things for the sole reason of being hurt. And as parents, we only do more harm by trying to keep them clutched instead of motivating and encouraging them to go for it. Instead, we should be the ones to offer them opportunities for growth and development, so they learn not to be bullied by their inner voices that keep putting them down.

In How Parents Can Raise Resilient Kids, we look at simple-to-follow, science-backed, and practical strategies and habits that will help parents raise mentally-strong, patient, and self-reliant kids. From helping them cope with uncertainties to failure and grief, we offer readers valuable insights to help kids overcome and recover from it. The book also features practical means to implement various strategies such as how to get them to become more confident, not fear making mistakes, take pride when owning up to them, and most important of all, learn to be resilient in tough times.

How Parents Can Raise Resilient Children

Preparing Your Child for the Real Tough World of Adulthood by Instilling Them With Principles of Love, Self-Discipline, and Independent Thinking

Frank Dixon

advice. The content within this book has been derived from various sources. Please consult a licensed professional before attempting any techniques outlined in this book.

By reading this document, the reader agrees that under no circumstances is the author responsible for any losses, direct or indirect, that are incurred as a result of the use of the information contained within this document, including, but not limited to, errors, omissions, or inaccuracies.

OTHER BOOKS BY FRANK DIXON

How Parents Can Raise Resilient Children:
Preparing Your Child for the Real Tough World of
Adulthood by Instilling Them With Principles of
Love, Self-Discipline, and Independent Thinking

❄ ❄ ❄

How Parents Can Teach Children To Counter
Negative Thoughts: Channelling Your Child's
Negativity, Self-Doubt and Anxiety Into
Resilience, Willpower and Determination

❄ ❄ ❄

How Parents Can Develop Happy Children:
Uplifting Ways to Build Your Kids Social Skills to
Transform Them Into Thriving and Successful
Adults

❄ ❄ ❄

How Parents Can Teach Children to Live With
Transparency: A Whole Heart Approach to
Effectively Raising Honest and Candid Kids
Without Secrets

❄ ❄ ❄

How Parents Can Foster Friendship in Children: Begin a Meaningful Relationship With Your Child as Both Parent and Friend Without the Power Struggle

❊ ❊ ❊

7 Vital Parenting Skills for Understanding Teenagers and Communicating with Teens: Proven Parenting Tips for Developing Healthy Relationships for Teens and Reducing Teen Anxiety

❊ ❊ ❊

7 Vital Skills for Parenting Teen Girls and Communicating with Your Teenage Daughter: Proven Parenting Tips for Raising Teenage Girls with Self-Confidence and Coping Skills

❊ ❊ ❊

7 Vital Parenting Skills for Teaching Kids With ADHD: Proven ADHD Tips for Dealing With Attention Deficit Disorder and Hyperactive Kids

❊ ❊ ❊

7 Vital Parenting Skills for Improving Child Behavior and Positive Discipline: Proven Positive Parenting Tips for Family Communication without Yelling or Negativity

❊ ❊ ❊

7 Vital Skills for Parenting Teen Boys and Communicating with Your Teenage Son: Proven Positive Parenting Tips for Raising Teenage Boys and Preparing Your Teenager for Manhood

❋ ❋ ❋

7 Effective Methods for Calming Kids Anxiety During the Covid-19 Pandemic: Easy Parenting Tips for Providing Your Kids Anxiety Relief and Preventing Teen Depression Caused by Coronavirus Isolation

❋ ❋ ❋

7 Proven Strategies for Parenting Toddlers that Excel, from Potty Training to Preschool: Positive Parenting Tips for Raising Toddlers with Exceptional Social Skills and Accelerated Learning Ability

❋ ❋ ❋

For a complete list, please visit

http://bestparentingbooks.org/books

YOUR FREE GIFT

Before we begin, I have something special waiting for you. Another action-paced book, free of cost. Think of it as my way of saying thank you to you for purchasing this.

Your gift is a special PDF actionable guide titled, **"Profoundly Positive Parenting: Learn the Top 10 Skills to Raising Extraordinary Kids!"**

As the title suggests, it's a collection of 10 parenting skills that will help you pave the way towards raising amazing and successful children. It's short enough to read quickly, but meaty enough to offer actionable advice that can make impactful changes to the way you parent.

Intrigued, I knew you would be!

Claim your copy of Profoundly Positive Parenting by clicking on the link below and join my mailing list:

http://bestparentingbooks.org/free-gift/

Before we jump in, I'd like to express my gratitude. I know this mustn't be the first book you came across and yet you still decided to give it a read. There are numerous courses and guides you could have picked instead that promise to make you an ideal and well-rounded parent while raising your children to be the best they can be.

But for some reason, mine stood out from the rest and this makes me the happiest person on the planet right now. If you stick with it, I promise this will be a worthwhile read.

In the pages that follow, you're going to learn the best parenting skills so that your child can grow to become the best version of themselves and in doing so experience a meaningful understanding of what it means to be an effective parent.

Notable Quotes About Parenting

"Children Must Be Taught How To Think, Not What To Think."

— Margaret Mead

"It's easier to build strong children than to fix broken men [or women]."

- Frederick Douglass

"Truly great friends are hard to find, difficult to leave, and impossible to forget."

– George Randolf

"Nothing in life is to be feared, it is only to be understood. Now is the time to understand more, so that we may fear less."

– Scientist Marie Curie

Table of Contents

Introduction

Sometimes, parenting is a lot like being in the war. You are the one leading the army into the unknown with a plan you have well-thought-of but still doubt. But what you forget to take into account is the enemy also has a plan that defies yours, and now you have to rethink your plan and strategies and devise a new one. But wait, the enemy gets the hint of it too and they are onto something mischievous themselves…

Ahh, this never ends. There are no martyrs and, at the end of the day, the enemy often sleeps better with their tummies full.

Parenting isn't easy and that is the nicest way to put it. It is walking in heels in the sand with a tray full of expensive champagne in it. It is finding that one sock in the whole house when you already have it on. You want silence and some peace, but you also know it means something suspicious is going on. You feel like you haven't bathed in years or worn heels or put on makeup and all these things, which, once were the norm now seem a luxury. There are no time-outs. It's a full-time job you joyously applied for and are now rethinking your mental state at that time. Plus, there are no paid leaves, vacations, bonuses, or even recognition for all the hard work you put in because that is just how cruel the world is.

It keeps pulling your leg over things you barely have control over and insists on declaring you a failure. And sometimes, it isn't someone from the outside; it is that inner voice that demotivates you and reminds you that you should do better the next time. But aren't we all trying our best already? It didn't seem that hard in the past, did it? Were we as crazy, hyperactive, and disobedient? Or was there something else that made us turn up this beautiful specimen? We weren't always nagging for things or crying over spilled milk (literally) and our parents never seemed to have any trouble raising us. Just a look of theirs and it would send shivers down our spine and we prayed to God to not be spanked the minute we got home.

Parenting has evolved over the years. We no longer have the same family structures and hierarchy. Our parents had help from their parents and relatives to raise us. We all lived nearby, and remember how they used to say, "It takes a whole village to raise a kid?" Well, it was very much like that. Kids were taught different values than the ones they are taught today. They were told to behave, stay disciplined, and be strong and tough. Today, they are taught to be more open, be active and inquisitive, and be whom they want to be. Don't get us wrong, there is no harm in any of these values but the way they are instilled upon kids is debatable.

Some parents give their kids complete liberty of writing their destiny, thinking they are smart to figure things out on their own. It may work for some, but most kids require direction and some disciplining. Discipline, bring synonymous to teaching and not punishment. They need a mentor, a role model, and a teacher to help them distinguish between right and wrong, help them build a strong character and face overwhelming emotions and challenges with self-control and logic. These are the virtues we, as parents, should bestow upon our kids. It is upon us to show them the path and then leave it up to them to decide when they want to start their journey and where they need to stop. We have to teach them to be independent, in control, resilient, and emotionally intellectual. Only then will they be ready for the tough world.

Together, in this book, we shall look at different ways to make kids ready for the competitive, ever-evolving, and challenging world that will pull them down if they are not resilient enough. Each chapter talks of a different value, the crucial role it plays in their development, and how kids can take them up with some help from their parents.

So, without further ado, let's get right into it, shall we?

Chapter 1:

Understanding Resilience

We have been using the word resilience for a long time now. It has different meanings in different applications. For instance, in biology, resilience is used to define the ability of an organism in an environment filled with predators and uncertainty. In ecology, researchers used the term to define an ecosystem's capacity to sustain its functions without being disturbed and, in case of any disturbance, returning to its natural/original state. In metallurgy, we use it to define a metal's property to resist when prone to shocks.

A French scientist, Boris Cyrulnik, first used the word to describe a human's ability to move on or carry on regardless of what trauma, breakdown, or failure it faced. So, in simpler terms, we can assume that resilience refers to having the ability to bounce back or not become affected by something after it has happened. It is about moving on and reconstructing ourselves post-shock or tragedy. Fortunately, it isn't a personality trait but rather a skill that can be nurtured and polished. Everyone has resilience. It is only a question of how much and whether we put it to good use or not when faced with trauma, failure, or tragedy. It doesn't mean that one doesn't find situations too intense, overwhelming, heartbreaking, or difficult to deal with. It is just how they respond to it and cope with it. People who are more resilient get over it quicker than those who aren't resilient enough.

As it is a skill, building or encouraging its use is achievable. It may take some time, effort, and patience, but it will happen. However, thinking that some significant change will happen overnight or after reading some inspirational book about it will make you resilient is fallacious. Whoever suggests this lacks knowledge or experience.

Embracing Resilience

The reason resilience in kids is becoming such a hot topic these days is because the world is becoming tougher by the day. There is more competition than ever and poor self-esteem and coping skills are not going to help them face it. They need to have the right direction, essential resources, and mental strength to find their place in it despite the challenges and hardships. They need to embrace and practice becoming resilient because things will only get harsher. But why resilience?

If we were to see what resilience in kids looks like, here are some characteristics they will hopefully possess. We shall let you decide if these are qualities you would want your kids to have or not.

Resilient children are socially adept. They know how to reach out to others for help such as caregivers, adults, or peers and establish stronger bonds with them. They find comfort in being social and are more open and communicative.

Resilient children possess more control of their emotions, feelings, and their reactions to those emotions and feelings. They have the leverage to influence situations and confront problems independently and confidently. They don't give up easily and continue to try and work on their inadequacies.

Resilient children are also optimistic. They don't face challenges with a cynical attitude. They are the ones who find something positive even amidst failures. For example, if forced to move cities and make new friends, a resilient kid won't feel shy or hold grudges against their parents. Instead, they will welcome the change positively and accept the new place and people open-heartedly. They feel fully prepared for whatever life throws at them and are excited rather than scared or worried when something challenging comes up.

Resilient children also believe their lives are purposeful. They don't see struggles or challenges as the reason to end it or give up hope. They set big goals in life, aren't afraid to follow their passions, and accept failure when it happens. For example, a kid who wants to stand first in class will work harder and give their best when it comes to assignments and projects even if they have a difficult time with them at the start.

Finally, resilient children also have great problem-solving skills. They don't hide their talents or skills and look for solutions to problems creatively and persistently. At the same time, they are also flexible in their attempts and don't always go by the book and take the required action. An example of this would be Casey, a three-year-old trying to open her toy basket. She doesn't give up after two attempts like her brother but continues to try to open the basket with every technique she can come up with. Ultimately, she kicks it hard enough so it falls on the ground and opens up itself. Yes, we know it isn't the best of examples as you will have to clean up the mess of all the toys on the carpet, but you have to appreciate the effort and technique.

The Need for Raising Resilient Kids

That being said, one simply can't overlook the benefits being resilient offers and the sooner you start with the principles, the better. When children are young, so are their minds. It isn't developed fully and thus able to absorb more and adapt. Did you know that by the time your kid starts kindergarten, 95% of their mind is fully developed? This means the sooner we begin with resilience-building habits, the better.

Besides, resilience doesn't stop them from trying new things or playing safe to avoid failure, heartbreak, or tragedy. It isn't meant to eliminate stress but rather, accept setbacks and pain as it comes. Just because someone is resilient doesn't mean they see the world with colored lenses. They just adapt to the aftermath better than others and learn to cope on their own. Like others, they experience grief and sadness that comes when they fight with their best friend, they too experience pain when they have to get flu shots at the doctor's, they too fear uncertainty when picking chits for who their science partner be... it is only that their mental outlook makes them competent to work through those difficult times and recover.

Therapist Joshua Miles has suggested some benefits of raising resilient kids which are worth giving a read. Take a look to convince yourself and your partner why you should start teaching them about resilience, even if they are just five years old. According to Miles, resilient kids:

- ! Show improved learning and greater academic achievement
- ! Take less offs from school due to sickness as they can recover sooner
- ! Demonstrate reduced risk-taking behaviors
- ! Are less likely to indulge in excessive drinking, using drugs, or smoking
- ! Have a lower mortality rate and better overall well-being and health
- ! Are family or community-oriented and empathic towards others

The Seven Cs of Building Resilience in Kids

Kenneth Ginsburg, a renowned pediatrician at the Philadelphia Children's Hospital believes every child tries to live up to the expectations we set for them. They are always looking up to adults who believe in their capabilities unconditionally and guide them with compassion and generosity. In his book, *Building Resilience and Children and Teens*, he talks about how all kids, young or old, require encouragement from their peers and parents to believe in the ideas they have and put them into practice. He further argues that if kids are only thinking about fitting in a box, they will never be able to think outside it, and thus, not do something extraordinary with their lives. They need to be encouraged and motivated to think in new ways and build resilience over time. He suggests using the seven Cs of resilience to raise them as mentally-tough and creative beings.

Competence

Children often seek recognition when they do something well. They want that clap and pat on the back from their parents and peers. Additionally, they also look for opportunities to cultivate new skills and foster talents. As parents, it is our job to provide them with ample opportunities to succeed and flourish. Here are some ideas on how you, as an adult, can help them develop competence:

- ●! Focus on the strengths they possess and not highlight their weaknesses
- ●! Tell them when they have made a mistake but in a positive manner. (I see you have accomplished the task well, but do you know if you had done it this way, it would have taken less time?)
- ●! Empower them to make their decisions themselves. Let them come up with solutions to a problem individualistically.
- ●! Don't suffocate them with your worry and concern. Of course, you want to protect them and keep them safe, but often when parents are too involved in a child's life, they start to feel incompetent. If there are things they can do themselves, let them handle them on their own.
- ●! Avoid comparing them with other siblings or kids their age.

Confidence

Your goal as a parent is to boost your child's talents and skills so they feel confident when attempting them. If they think you believe they can hit the ball out of the court, they might do it. Why? Because they feel confident! That confidence is a product of your faith and belief in their skills and abilities that makes them push for things that are sometimes unachievable. Here are some ways you can build confidence in them:

- ●! Focus on the best things about your child's personality so they start to see that as well
- ●! Teach them about fairness, persistence, integrity, and kindness
- ●! Avoid pushing them to do something they are not comfortable attempting or feel like they can't handle it
- ●! Praise honestly like you mean it when they achieve something – even if it is the hundredth time they do it

Connection

Children want to feel like they belong somewhere. They want to feel like they aren't alone and want to cultivate meaningful connections with everyone if given the chance. Therefore, as parents, it is your job to not push them away when they come to us with their problems or struggles with something. To help them build connections with everyone around them without hesitance or fear of being disregarded, here's what you need to do:

- ●! Ensure they are safe and always looked after physically
- ●! Allow them the liberty to be as expressive as they want to be when it comes to big emotions. For instance, don't ask them to quiet down

when they are upset about something or feel like crying. Instead, offer them ideas on how they can cope with what they are feeling in more productive ways

●! Resolve problems as they arise by addressing conflict openly

●! Make your house welcoming to all forms of communication. Designate an area where the family can share time and have a decent conversation

●! Foster healthy relationships that promote positive messages

Character

Every kid needs a moral compass to follow and a basic understanding of what's right and what's not. This shows them they can't be put down for who they are. To build a strong character in them, begin with:

●! Showing them they are empathetic and caring

●! Demonstrating how negative behaviors can sometimes cloud judgment and make things difficult

●! Preaching the importance of community and the perks of helping others

●! Eliminating stereotyping or racial discriminations and raising them as morally-sound

Contribution

Kids are naturally empathetic. They will come to comfort you when they see you upset. It is their natural tendency to contribute in some way. Therefore, when they come to you and present you with a get well soon card or a hug, don't disregard them. They want to be of service and even if you think you need to be alone, let them know politely. When they feel valued, they will continue to be of help. They also learn how good it feels to be able to help and don't feel shy asking for it either. This is one important aspect of becoming resilient – that you seek help without any shame or guilt. Here's how you can encourage them to contribute more:

- •! Communicate with them how many people in the world lack necessities like food and shelter so they learn to be compassionate and not act privileged
- •! Stress how important it is to be of service to others
- •! Model generosity yourself and always choose to discipline with empathy (more on this is the next chapter)
- •! Create opportunities that allow them to contribute or ask for their help with the chores so they learn to contribute innately

Coping

Children also need to learn some coping mechanisms against stress, so they know when to engage or disengage themselves from things and people. When they learn better coping mechanisms, they will be more prepared to face adversity and ultimately get over it. Below are a few ways to teach them how to cope better:

- ! Model positive coping strategies as kids learn what they see
- ! Teach them how to implement coping strategies consistently such as what to do when they feel angry, sad, or emotionally-troubled
- ! Understand that whatever negative behavior your child is depicting is due to some underlying stress about something and, therefore, be empathetic.
- ! Understand that telling them to stop that negative behavior is only going to make matters worse, and therefore, try to distract them in some other way so they become engaged elsewhere.

Control

Children who are aware they are the ones in control of their decisions are likelier to bounce back after something tragic. When they feel in control, they know that whatever they choose to do is their own doing, and thus, no one else should be blamed but them. This type of behavior is also prominent in adults. When we think our mistakes are our own, we face them willingly. We know it was no one's doing but our own that failed, and thus, we are quick to pick up ourselves. As parents, we can encourage the same in the following manner:

●! Help them comprehend that everything happening to them isn't purely random whilst also teaching them that not everything is under our control, and therefore, we shouldn't hold ourselves accountable all the time.

●! Also, use discipline and compassion to teach them anything new. They don't need to see you controlling or punishing you because they will adopt the same behavior.

Chapter 2:

All Kids Are Independent

Thinkers

According to Linda S. Gottfredson, an education professor at the University of Delaware, intelligence reflects how we process information, learn, understand, and reason things (Gottfredson, 1996). There is no means to tell that a kid with its head submerged in books will be smarter than the one roaming the streets. There is no means to measure how they process new information, what they learn from it, and how they make use of that newfound knowledge.

This is why some kids are street-smart while others enjoy the reading bit. It is why some of them are interested in painting pictures and others in building towers with blocks. It is why some kids are the school's favorite footballers while some are everyone's friend and know how to make others feel better.

Every child is unique and creative in their ways, and as adults, it is our job to hone that creativity and uniqueness in them so they can find a place for themselves in this world. It is our job to encourage and motivate them to follow their passions and not force them into doing or taking up things they aren't interested in. There is little chance your son will do well with cello lessons if all he wants is to play soccer. It is less likely that someone who doesn't like ballet will be good at it. Therefore, as parents, the first thing you need to do is stop comparing your kids to someone else. They are unique in their way and thus don't need to be bullied or forced to go to that next practice session if they want to take up the stage and become a performer. Just because someone else's kid is doing it doesn't mean yours have to, too.

Even though we know that comparison doesn't sit well with everyone, it is especially debasing for little ones. Kids are tender and less emotionally-intelligent when young. They don't adhere well to criticism, especially when it comes to people they trust the most. There is always some better way of telling them to improve or do better than rubbing their face in their shortcomings or mistakes.

Many parents argue that it is quite natural to want to know where their kids stand amongst others and what percentages they have or what ranks they hold so when the time comes to bid for a coveted seat in a top university, they know they aren't making a fool of themselves. True, but does that mean you get the right to parade them in front of others like decorative pieces and ask them to show off their skill and harangue them when they don't do well? This is the very practice that makes them develop an inferiority complex. Other than that:

Comparison leads to the kid withdrawing themselves from others and social gatherings (Rubin, Coplan, & Bowker, 2009). They create this idea in their head that no matter how hard they try, someone will upstage them and outperform, so there is no point in trying and becoming a laughing stock.

It also causes self-doubt where the kids start to question if they will ever be anything but average or not. They feel there is nothing they can excel at and thus give up before even trying.

Secondly, it lowers their self-esteem and eats away their confidence. They start to question their self-worth when they don't think of themselves as good enough. They feel like they lack the abilities and skills other kids their age have. These lead to unwanted stress and depression in their lives and ultimately lead to multiple mental health issues at a young age (Solomons, 2013).

Thirdly, it lays roots of jealousy and rivalry. When being compared to an apparent paragon of virtue incessantly, they develop hatred and jealousy towards them. Jealousy is never a positive expression and thus must never be cultivated. It can lead to aggressiveness in kids.

And finally, it suppresses their talents and skills. When they are not appreciated for who they are and what makes them unique, their talents don't blossom either and they eventually lose them.

So, treat them with kindness and compassion so they can confidently put their skills and talents to good use.

Putting the C in Creativity

Many researchers today believe it is our doing that kids are no longer creative. Wondering why they think such a thing? Well, ask yourself this: when you were little, did you have as many toys as kids of today have? Did they spend all their time confined in homes or glued to screens for hours without notice? Even though the goal of toy companies is to improve the overall experience of play for kids, they are unintentionally reaping them off their imagination. Children no longer indulge in pretend-play and make-believe games. They have everything in the palm of their hands already. The same can be said for adolescents and teenagers. Just a swipe on their phones and they are introduced to all the knowledge and entertainment in the world there is.

Kids have powerful imaginations but, like a car engine, they need proper fueling. This feeling comes in the form of encouragement and believes in their abilities. Since the goal is to help them develop resilience, we had to look and find if there was a connection between creativity and resilience or not. Interestingly, there is.

According to one study, kids who are more creative thinkers cope with pain and stress better (Reznick, 2009). They are more confident in their approaches to deal with any hardship and challenge, have better social skills that enable them to seek guidance and help, and are better learners and problem-solvers.

So, how do you cultivate creativity if that is what makes them resilient? Here are a few ideas worth trying.

Offer them the resources they need to express their creative side. Give them an ample amount of unstructured time for imaginative play. Secondly, give them space both physical and mental to attempt things independently. Don't mind creative clutter. Let them pull out every toy from the basket, stay in their rooms or up in the attic playing and imagining things.

Let curiosity be their guide and take them to new places. Encourage their intrigue to know more about any and everything. Take them to places that will broaden their knowledge like museums. Don't shush them up when they bother you with a million "whys."

Most importantly, never underestimate, mock, or dismiss their ideas. No idea is ever a stupid one. Mocking or ridiculing an idea discredits their creativity and they may feel incompetent. Their idea may be bogus but it can still hold some merit in terms of the concept, thought process, or rationale. Work with them to polish and nurture it with them.

Avoid acting bossy or trying to modify their ideas by adding your touch to them. Kids don't need that. Give them the freedom and autonomy to explore them on their own. If they want to go to every neighbor's house to feed their dog because they want to, don't tell them it isn't safe and clutch them to your chest fearing their safety. Instead, ask them if they would like you to accompany them and hold the treats for them. If the

Are you authoritative?

Finally, we have authoritative parenting, which is slightly different than both parenting styles mentioned above. Authoritative parents are those who set firm limits, have some room for healthy discussion, and realize it is their job to teach self-discipline. So, they allow their children to do whatever they want to do but also tell them the consequences of their actions. For example, telling your child to go to bed early so they don't miss the school bus and walk to school is authoritative parenting. You are giving them the choice to pick a certain behavior but also telling them where it would lead them. It involves teaching them to be their boss but also facing the consequences of their actions and owning up to them when the time comes. This is what makes them self-disciplined and resilient, don't you think?

But why do we discipline kids in the first place? Is it because we want them to give up certain behaviors? Is it because we want them to excel at everything in their future? Is it because we want to teach them the difference between right and wrong or good or bad?

Most parents discipline their kids because they want them to grow up as responsible, wise, and honest adults. But before we learn of the many techniques to discipline that doesn't involve punishments, we need to understand why kids misbehave.

Children often misbehave, disobey, or disregard their parents' advice because they feel emotionally-stimulated. They feel too much and too often and don't know what to make of those feelings. They feel jealous when another sibling gets more attention, they feel frustrated and angry when being compared with others, and they feel upset because they feel unheard and uncared for. As they are young, their limbic system is developed more than their frontal cortex, which regulates emotions. This means the emotions they feel are stronger than what their minds can handle or cope with. Their frontal cortex only starts developing when they pass toddlerhood.

Setting Limits and Consequences Without Punishments

Now that we understand some of what goes on inside their tiny heads, we continue from where we left off – techniques that discipline kids without punishing them. The reason we insist on positive disciplining is that when kids are faced with big emotions and don't know what to do about them, they do what they know: cry, throw a tantrum, or become aggressive. We perceive these actions as an act of misbehavior and become too rigid and harsh. Kids can start to fear such a response, which is something no parent wants. So, when it comes to disciplining them, here are some ideas to take note of.

Be Their Role Model

They need to learn to regulate their emotions and act resiliently in difficult times. And who can teach them better than their parents? But the question is: what do you do when faced with hardships? Because believe it or not, chances are your kids are going to pick up the same response. Therefore, if you have the habit of yelling, screaming, cursing, and isolating yourself in times of hardship, your kids are going to do that too. So, the first rule is to learn to self-regulate your emotions. They need to understand that emotions are natural and shouldn't be hidden or run away from. They allow us to set boundaries by determining what we are okay with and with what we aren't.

Nourish the Parent-Child Relationship

No matter how young or old your kids are, they will always come to you with their problems. They may not be too forward when they are older, but their changed behavior is a sign that something isn't right. Therefore, for parents, it is imperative that a strong parent-child relationship is built from an early age so the child views their parents as their mentor and guide. Kids will always try their hardest to impress you. They will rarely deliberately try to disappoint you. Multiple research studies suggest that when a strong parent-child relationship is prevalent, kids are less likely to misbehave. It isn't fear of their anger that makes them well-behaved but rather the sanctity of the special bond. They don't want to do anything that would upset the stability of the bond. This connection has to be fostered with care in terms of soothing, connecting with them frequently, and correcting them with empathy.

Be Their Behavior Mentor

Just a made-up word, but what it stands for is important. If you wish to instill discipline, you have to be more loving and caring. Kids are more receptive when spoken to with love and treated with care and interest. Their brains blank out the minute they are scolded by their parents or teachers. This eliminates the need for it as it doesn't guarantee any favorable results. It is a universal fact that when we are stressed out, our brain stops to process new information clearly and we are less likely to make sane decisions.

Love Can Go a Long Way

If you take a look at all those studies done on resilient people, you will be surprised to know that many of them rated companionship of someone who trusted in them and stood by them without judgment the highest. As kids look up their parents and peers, they seek acceptance and recognition. They want to be cared for, loved, and heard. It is very difficult to love one's self if no one else does. So, surrounding yourself with people who love you, accept you, and correct you without being accusatory and judgmental is essential. You always turn to them in times of adversity and are assured they will come to your rescue. When we feel safe or understand what it feels like, we develop an optimistic outlook. We become more caring and devoted to others. We want to support others too and be there for them in times of need. We take into account what they are going through and offer aid and compassion.

This is what empathy is all about. Teaching something new with empathy and love is more likely to stick with them. Picture this: your child is going through a rough patch. They have just broken up with their best friend and are worried if they will ever talk to them again. Instead of being negative or judgmental, if you decide to be empathetic, sit them down, and try to be in their shoes when offering solutions, it will be received well. On the other hand, if you treat them with condescending views or disregard their problem as something petty, there is little chance they will come to you the next time.

Thus, reaching out to them with empathy is what seems like an ideal solution whether you are trying to treat misbehavior, negative emotions, or instill new habits. How can being empathetic make you a better teacher to stem new habits like resilience, self-discipline, and independence? Let's see!

Implanting New Habits With Love and Empathy

Be a Coach, But Don't Coach

Sounds confusing, but hear us out. You want them to obey you, follow your commands, and take up good habits but not while you order them to. Coaches help children develop and enhance skills, but it is they who have to play the game and show how well they have been taught. As a parent, you have to act as their mentor and teach them rather than doing things for them. The only way to build resilience is if they have confidence in themselves to get over things. Don't rob them of the opportunity to learn competence.

Aim for Progress and Not Perfection

If it is something new you are teaching them, don't expect them to become masters of it overnight. Teaching new habits like resilience, emotional-intelligence, and independence take time and effort. So, don't push too hard, and aim for progress and improvement. Too much pressure can undermine their confidence.

Teach Independence by Allowing Them to be Independent

Many teachers believe the best way to teach someone something new is to let them experience it hands-on. You can't learn to swim if you are afraid of the water.

Don't abandon them completely but encourage trying new things. Stay back and watch from a distance how well or poorly they do it. Offer aid only when asked and don't forget to appreciate it.

Empathize and Praise Descriptively

Instead of just saying, "Good job," give them something more and meaningful to be happy about. Tell them what they did well and why you think it was brilliant. Descriptive praise helps hone all those areas they are experts in. Also, don't forget to empathize and appreciate accordingly. Tell them how proud you are they pulled XYZ off and how hard it must have been for them. Tell them how happy you are they didn't give up and strived to become better.

Chapter 3:

Taking Responsibility

Do you recall the first time you held them in your arms? You swore to yourself that you will let no harm come to them. Ever since then, you have loved them unconditionally, watched them grow, cried with them when they were hurt, played nonsensical games with them for hours, worried about their health, nutrition, and well-being, helped them crawl, stand, and walk on their two feet, and offered them comfort and your warm embrace whenever they came crying to you over something. As parents, we all want to nurture our kids, keep them safe from harm, and teach them the best values so when they grow up, they are ready for the world.

But amidst doing so, we have, and we are talking about every parent here, sometimes shielded them from making mistakes. We have been to the rescue before they did something wrong or harmful. Although you aren't to blame here, did you know that whenever you did that, you deprived them of a great learning opportunity to grow and build resilience (Oosthuizen, 2020)? To raise them as healthy, capable, emotionally-intellectual, and confident individuals, we have to let them make mistakes. But, of course, own up to them too!

When do children make mistakes? When they do something the way it shouldn't have been done. Usually, errors result in failure, which leads to stress and the buildup of negative emotions. But despite that, children must be given every opportunity to struggle so even if they fail, they develop emotional and coping skills. Many psychologists associate coping skills as muscles. We can never know how strong we are unless we use them.

Historically, many educators believed that to perfect one's development of skills, the best way was to eliminate the creation of mistakes. It made sense for some time and many other educators followed suit too but things started to change when researchers and child specialists observed how crucial a role mistakes play in fostering resilience. Even today, we don't deliberately set up our kids for failure. We have this premeditated notion to make things easier for them so they can do without making mistakes. Unconsciously, we all discourage mistakes as we feel it is synonymous with failure. So, we drill the right answers into them by repeating the question over and over again until they memorize it and pray that they do well in a standardized test too. Because God forbid, who can afford poor grades even though the child has zero knowledge about the concepts and foundation of things?

Recent studies suggest that learning improves when kids make mistakes as their curiosity to know what is right is heightened. Every form of learning is enriched via error. Ask yourself this: if they won't choose the wrong friends first, how will they know how to choose the right ones? If they won't wear the left shoe in their right foot and fall, how will they know to put the right shoe in the right foot the next time? Making mistakes challenges kids to do better. Rarely do mistakes result in them giving up. Mistakes motivate them to think differently, come up with a new possible solution or explanation for things. It makes their mind go in turbo-charge mode to attempt things differently. Isn't that what learning should look like? It should be fun, challenging, and a driving force to discover new possibilities and approaches.

According to Carol Dweck, the author of the bestseller, *Mindset: The New Psychology of Success* and a professor at Stanford University, children must always be challenged one way or another to enhance learning. Even when they repeatedly make mistakes, parents' shouldn't try to make things easier for them and rather let them come up with new strategies and means to handle them. Did you know, her research suggests that when parents repetitively praise children for their intelligence rather than their problem-solving skills, they are less likely to remain persistent in the face of a challenge? This conclusion was derived after her team of experts followed up with 100+ 5th graders in the best schools of NYC. In her book, she writes about the experiment in detail to encourage parents to praise kids over their efforts − even if they fail − and not their intelligence, which happens to be a genetic trait. To briefly sum up her experiment, she divided the participating 5th graders into two groups. One group was appreciated for their intelligence while the other for their effort.

As it turns out, when faced with a challenging test designed for 8th graders, children who were praised for their efforts performed harder despite making numerous mistakes. They seemed more determined to take on the task and tried their best to perform better. On the other hand, children who were praised for their intelligence were soon to feel like a failure as the more mistakes they made, the more discouraged they got.

This proved that parents who praised results more than efforts don't raise resilient kids. Instead, what they raise are kids who are too scared to disappoint that they don't even give their best shot at things. Therefore, if you are doing the same, you can't expect them to grow up to become resilient as they lack the skills to accept failure and come out of it. Moreover, Dweck also believes parents shouldn't be too quick to praise or put down their children as they lose important opportunities for learning.

Did I Do Something Wrong?

A mistake can be anatomized as a decision or action we soon come to regret. Mistakes come paired with some form of loss, pain, and struggle. No one, not even adults are in favor of what consequences it brings along. But that doesn't mean we never make one. We all do! Sometimes, graver than the ones made by our kids. But the irony is that mistakes are one of the things we try hard not to stumble upon and yet sometimes, also the most important things we need to experience.

As we don't like to be reminded of our mistakes from time to time, so do our kids. Parents who have the habit of bringing up their children's mistakes in front of others to joke or ridicule them are setting them up for poor self-worth and low self-esteem. Kids who are often mocked by one or both their parents exhibit unstable mental health as they feel they are not good enough. As parents, we shouldn't bring up past mistakes to degrade our kids as no one likes to deliberately make them. Besides, as we have already established that making mistakes can be good; we have to format our responses accordingly.

Watching our kids make a blunder is never easy. Knowing that what they are doing is wrong, it is hard to resist the temptation of making things better for them. Of course, your instinct is to save them from trauma, pain, or hurt later, but perhaps it is best to let them navigate their way themselves. When they spring back from mistakes with techniques they came up with, it boosts their sense of confidence in their abilities.

So, instead of focusing solely on what they did wrong, we should try to focus on helping them cope with the emotions that follow after. How will they cope with anger, frustration, or guilt after they have made a mistake? Well, that is where you step in. But before we do that, make sure you do the following:

Say Thank You

If they come up to you to admit they have made a boo-boo, thank them for it. Of course, it will boil your blood when they tell you what they have done but this is the moment when you have to overlook their mistake and praise them for their honesty. This gives children an open window for communication as they feel they can come up to you with whatever troubles them and be expressive about it. This also teaches them you will offer help rather than a sound scolding, which instills the idea that they always have someone they can count on.

Encourage Risk-Taking

Your kid should be trying something new every day to broaden their knowledge and learning. They shouldn't worry about making mistakes or becoming scared of failure. Show them it is okay to step out of their comfort zones and give new things a try.

Be Vocal About Their Efforts

If you have only been praising them over an A+ grade or win in the spelling bee contest, you are amplifying their fears of trying new things. They start to believe that if they try something new, they will surely fail. This makes them dependent and less resilient. So, applaud their efforts even if they fail to achieve the desired results. This will make them persistent and more willing to take on new challenges without the fear of failure.

Tell Them a Secret

To instill the habit of owning up to their mistakes, share with them mistakes you made when you were their age and how you coped with them. Tell them in detail how you handled them, owned up them, and made required compensations to prevent repeating them. When kids make mistakes, they feel like failures. They think they are incapable of handling things. But having someone tell them they aren't the only ones to make mistakes drills a sense of comfort in them and gives them a boost to do better.

Teach Them Accountability

One of the greatest things one can do when they have faulted is to accept responsibility for their actions and be accountable. In case our mistakes have hurt someone, it is our job to apologize and pay our condolences. Your kids should be taught the same from an early age so they learn an important life lesson – fixing something that has been broken at the right time. They must acknowledge that their actions resulted in someone getting hurt and therefore, it is now their job to make amends. This also allows them to move past the grief, shame, and guilt they feel. It also shows them that everything can be made better if one tries hard enough.

Teach Them to Trace Back

Kids need to know what mistakes they made and where. If you want them to claim responsibility for their blunders, ask them what they did and what happened afterward. The second part of the sentence is to remind them to trace back and know what action resulted in the mistake, so the next time, they avoid repeating it.

Tell Them What's Done Is Done

There is no point holding onto the faults. Kids shouldn't think that just because they have made a mistake, it is the end of the world. Instead, tell them it is just the beginning of learning. For example, if they lost a race on sports day, instead of putting them down, encourage them to try harder the next time, get a coach, or try a different technique. But be mindful as you don't want to hand them the solutions on a plate; you need to encourage them to brainstorm ideas themselves.

Be Their Accountability Partner

If you want them to avoid repeating the same mistakes over and over again, someone has to keep them in check and navigate their way with them. Be their accountability partner so you remain aware that they haven't fully given up something because they made a blunder the last time and also to remind them to work harder as you are counting on them. Create chore lists and place them in visible places where they can see them. Be sure to mention the mistake they made the last time in a subtle but clear manner. For example, if the last time they forgot to separate their laundry in white and blacks, a little reminder suggesting to sort properly can go a long way.

Chapter 4:

Managing Big Feelings

Mentally-strong and resilient kids are in control of their feelings and emotions. They know how to remain sane and take critical decisions at the right time without letting their emotions and internal feelings cloud their judgment. They know how to regulate them accordingly. They don't let their emotions overpower them or become the controller. As this looks like a favorable skill, it is ideal to develop it in your kids too. They too should know how to handle their reactions and form better responses. They too should know how to keep negative emotions at bay.

But here is where the problem lies. Kids aren't born with an understanding of emotions. Their lack of vocabulary further escalates the problem as they aren't able to put into words what they are going through. So, to expect them to be socially-appropriate when expressing themselves is a little too much to ask. This is one reason why child specialists and counselors suggest starting as early as possible to build resilience. So, when they are faced with a challenging situation or emotion, they know how to handle it appropriately.

When children aren't taught to self-regulate their emotions and manage their responses and behaviors, they often resort to aggressive behaviors to have their demands fulfilled. However, when they are denied that liberty, they bring out the angry face and start to throw things or create a scene. This portrays bad parenting. Besides, no child should be left to feel sad all by themselves for hours at a time over some small loss like the death of their best caterpillar. No matter how big the challenge or hardship, they should know how to handle it.

Another reason why learning to regulate emotions is essential is because when kids don't understand what they are experiencing, they avoid feeling that way. They start to avoid situations that will yield similar emotions. This fear of attempting anything outside of their comfort zones can limit their potential to soar high and be prepared to fly away from the nest, aka be prepared for the tough world outside. For instance, someone who doesn't do well in big social circles will try their best to avoid interactions as they don't feel comfortable. When the same kid starts school or heads for college, they will never be the first ones to raise their hand despite knowing the answer to a question or join an activity with lots of classmates. Their lack of confidence and fear of being social will limit their chances of success.

Feelings can be overwhelming, even for adults. Imagine how hard it must be for our little ones. They are still only learning so much every minute of the day, and being introduced to some foreign emotion, it can become challenging, to say the least.

Developing Coping Skills

Without the self-regulation of emotions, kids are going to act out. They are just being kids by saying, "Since we feel out of control, we shall act like it too." Therefore, strong coping skills should be harnessed to make them independent and self-reliant. Kids who aren't taught how to manage emotions the right way learn it themselves and they aren't always guaranteed to be the best. For instance, some adults fall into the habit of drinking and drug addiction because they are unable to cope with how they feel. They resort to self-harming practices that further take them down the dark pit. No parent in their right mind would want to see their kid grow up to be like that. Therefore, to avoid the chances of them picking up unhealthy coping strategies, be the torchbearer they need in their lives to navigate the way.

It is also observed that children with unhealthy coping mechanisms also exhibit avoidance coping. Avoidance coping can be defined as avoiding one activity and indulging in another to make oneself feel better. If we were to see an example of it, it would look something like this: a child ditching their homework to go outside and play ball with their friends because they don't possess the requisite problem-solving skills to do it. So, they avoid the activity altogether because playing ball makes them feel more relaxed and in control. Just because they didn't try to learn to handle their anxiety around math homework, they are willing to further fall behind in school.

According to one study, kids who use avoidance coping are at a higher risk of using marijuana as they grow up (Hyman & Sinha, 2008). Those who lack the basic problem-solving skills and are ready to put their hands up in the air and surrender showed lifetime marijuana use. This shows that the lack of proper coping strategies can lead to dependence on life-threatening things like substance abuse.

On a positive note, children who develop strong coping skills are more resilient in general and enjoy better opportunities in life. They have better overall well-being and are more social and empathetic in nature as opposed to those who haven't developed the right coping strategies (Jones, Greenberg, & Crowley, 2015). The same study also suggested that kids who had learned to regulate their emotions at the supple age of five were more likely to enroll in college and have steady high-paying jobs. They are also less likely to indulge in criminal activities, report mental health problems, and/or become engaged in substance abuse.

Strategies to Manage Riotous Emotions at an Early Age

Whether you accept it or not, no matter how coveted you try to keep your children, they will experience heartaches, hurt, jealousy, and guilt. Feeling emotions is a certainty no one can escape from. Despite trying to omit and avoid circumstances that are tough and challenging, they will routinely come in contact with them. Since there is not much to control, there is no point in trying to. What you can do, however, is to acknowledge as to what degree these emotions affect their behavior and actions. You have the power to teach them to control their responses to those feelings and learn to regulate them over time. This will help them grow both emotionally and mentally. Coping strategies help the user recognize what emotions they are feeling and how to better address them. Once they address them, they can cultivate an appropriate response to them.

Teaching coping skills will also help them relate to others better and shape their behavior in different situations. The more expressive and understanding they are of their behavior, the better your relationship with them will be. Instead of acting out in frustration or anger, they will express them in manners that are suitable and apposite.

So, how can we teach them and, more importantly, what should we be teaching them? Let's learn together.

The first thing you need to do is help them give that feeling a name. If they are too young, they may not know what terms like "happy, sad, angry" mean. If they are older and school-going, they might interpret their feelings incorrectly. For instance, they may be feeling guilt but interpret it as sadness. As a parent, it is your job to help them identify the feelings and the best way to do so is by labeling it.

The next thing you need to do is identify triggers. What causes a certain feeling? What makes them react in a certain way? Your children should know about the cause and effect reaction. They must be sound enough to identify the things that trigger a certain behavior so they can avoid being in those situations or face them with enhanced confidence.

Tell them it is alright and there is no need to lash out uncontrollably. Often small kids take to throwing tantrums and whining when told "no." When that happens, you have to empathize with them and tell them that what they are experiencing is normal and that you would have been frustrated too if that were to happen to you. However, the goal should be to teach them the right and wrong way of expression. If they are going through something, they should willingly learn to manage it on their own. This develops a sense of independence in them. Let them know they must be cautious of their reactions and words irrespective of the situation.

Once they understand, introduce them to some basic strategies to cope with the emotions they are feeling. For example, if they are feeling down about something, offer some distracting ideas that would uplift their mood. Perhaps suggesting things like going to the park or for a drive or calling up their friend or favorite cousin to cheer up are all great ideas to cope.

Next, don't make the mistake of trying to fix things for them. All children must be encouraged to learn to work through their things independently. We know you hate seeing them sad and know that with a flick of a hand, you can make things better for them. But don't. This is necessary for two reasons: a) they are growing older and less dependent on you and after some time, you won't be able to manipulate the world for them and b) you have to make them learn to cope with uncertainty and unpredictability because, let's face it, life isn't always fair.

And finally, teach them to regulate their emotions using calming techniques so they don't lose their mind over something trivial. Introduce some deep breathing techniques so they can learn to control the urge to react immediately and without thinking straight. Ask them to breathe in and breathe out and make sure to hold their breath for a good 2 to 5 seconds before exhaling the air. Repeat this up to 10 times or more until they calm down and have a grasp on themselves.

If they are continuously distracted by upsetting thoughts like the ones we used to get before the teacher announced the final year results, tell them to start counting. This works well for everyone, even in the time of crisis. If they are in the car, ask them to count how many cars take over; if they are in the playground or social event, ask them to count how many people are wearing a certain color; if they are in the house, ask them to roam around and see how many paintings or frames are hung up in the house.

You can DIY a calming-kit containing their favorite snacks, leisure activity, or books they like to read. It can be crayons and a coloring book, paints, a favorite lotion or perfume, a car set, or soothing tunes they enjoy listening to. All these will not only cheer them up but also allow them to learn that every negative emotion can be turned into something positive.

Tell them they can ask for a time-out or small break if they aren't feeling too well. This could be a minute or 10 to recollect and gather their thoughts before they turn to anxiety and panic. During this time, tell your child to calm down, have a sip of water, and take deep breaths.

Chapter 5:

Time to Toughen Up!

Enough talk about it already; in this chapter, we are going to dive straight into the techniques and strategies that will enable you to raise your kids as resilient, confident, self-disciplined, and self-reliant adults. Most of these strategies are backed by years of experiments and research studies, which are a testament of how productive they are.

Try Strength-Based Parenting

According to Lea Waters, a professor at the University of Melbourne, strength-based parenting focuses on the identification and cultivation of positive states, qualities of your child, and processes they go through when faced with a certain situation. Think of it as an addition of a positive filter on parenting that aids parents in teaching kids how to react to stress. This eliminates the chance(s) of kids using aggressive coping reactions or complete avoidance to run away from a stressful situation.

During a preliminary study, Walter and her colleagues explored this newfound concept with a group of primary-school-age children in Australia's middle schools (Waters, 2015). The participating kids were presented with a stressful scenario such as breaking up with a friend over some small fight or being the only student in the class to not have completed an assignment due the next day. The kids are asked to discuss their responses. The majority of the kids came up with negative responses such as freaking out, being depressed, or getting angry. Only a handful of them listed some positive means to cope with the proposed situation. They came up with responses like breathing techniques to get over something faster and reminding themselves of all the good times they had spent with that friend. They also indicated their parents appreciated their strengths and encouraged them to use these kinds of techniques in times of stress to deal with it better.

This suggests that parents who focus more on the skills and strengths of their children rather than pulling them down for their weaknesses are also those who teach them to cope better with stress.

Problem-Solve With Them

Not many parents are aware of the fact that their words hold immense value in the way kids express themselves. If they are reluctant and less open to communication, their kids will refrain from coming to them to discuss how they are feeling. As a result, they may take up unhealthy coping strategies and cause further harm to themselves in the future. Therefore, be communicative and offer problem-solving ideas. Encourage them to think of ways to overcome a certain situation or challenge instead of telling them what to do exactly. Some responses can be:

- •! What do you think we should do right now?
- •! Can you tell me how I can make you feel better right now?
- •! When you faced a similar situation before, what worked for you?
- •! Can you fill me in with what is going inside your head?
- •! What can you do to get out of this mess?

Notice how none of these statements offers solutions but rather encourage your kid to come up with one on their own.

Introduce Self-Discipline

Remember the ever-so-famous marshmallow effect? Here's a little reminder if you aren't able to recall the years old test for delayed gratification and self-discipline. Psychologist Walter Mischel called in a few kindergarteners for a test that involved marshmallows. In front of them, each child had a plate containing one marshmallow. The researcher was then called in by someone (planned) but before leaving the room, the researcher made a simple request. If the child wants, they can have the marshmallow right away, but if they waited for the researcher to come back, they will have two. The request was simple but portrayed something very deep within us. It showed how we all are prisoners of instant gratification. Many kids ate the marshmallow without waiting for the researcher. But those who didn't and showed remarkable self-discipline even at such an early age went on to have greater academic scores, better careers, and healthier relationships than their counterparts.

Coming back to the point, every parent must teach their children principles of self-discipline, so they learn to behave appropriately, even when overwhelmed by emotions. The best way to teach a kid that is to make them understand the perks of distraction from temptations. Surely, you may feel like crying a river in the supermarket because the store is out of your favorite gummy bears, but you have to behave and act better. This also builds resilience.

Allow Them to Take Calculated Risks

Be clear when telling them their courage and willingness to fight back and manage emotions is far more commendable than the outcome they achieve. Help them find their freedom to make choices and take decisions so even when they make mistakes, they have no one to blame but themselves. We already established in earlier chapters how this benefits them in the long run. Freedom will facilitate them in knowing what their triggers are, how they can navigate their emotions better, and how to cope with the things that aren't in one's control. They should always be encouraged to take risks and try new things so when they fail, they can learn to get over it and move on. If they won't try anything new, they will spend their whole life in a predictable manner and lose their calm the minute something odd happens. Therefore, it is better to prepare them for uncertainty beforehand.

Avoid Shielding Them From Stress

According to Dennis Charney, a psychiatrist at the Icahn School of Medicine, children who have been through some traumatic experience in their life such as the loss of a parent or loved one, suffered domestic assault, been hit by some natural disaster or been jailed, do better than those who hasn't been through something like that. They portray improved coping skills in difficult times as opposed to those who have had things handed to them with ease.

She explained why such kids are better at bouncing back and healing faster. She believes that since kids who have been through some traumatic incidents have faced challenges right in their faces instead of avoiding their existence or reality, they emerged stronger. For parents, this means engaging kids in challenging tasks, so they learn to cope better and make sense of what is happening instead of running in the other direction. But don't get us wrong, this doesn't mean leaving them in a forest to find their way back home or in an empty parking lot. It is about exposing them to controlled stressful situations that makes them come up with a plan to get out of them. When kids are left on their own to deal with their problems, they develop a psychological toolbox of coping strategies that come in handy when they are adults.

Foster Optimism

Research suggests that optimism is one of the chief traits of resilient people (Ong, et al., 2006). They see the grass greener on both sides, know that the glass is filled (not half-filled or half-empty), and live with a positive outlook towards life. Optimism kills stress and we don't need to provide you with facts to convince you. Therefore, as parents, you must try to nurture optimism by exposing your kids to experiences that make them happier. This doesn't mean you go on invalidating the way they feel but rather presenting them with opportunities that makes them see life as beautiful and worthy. To help them cope with an existing emotion, try to find something positive in it. For example, if your child had been planning for weeks for a school trip and for some reason it got canceled at the last minute, take them someplace they enjoy going to so they understand that all is never lost.

The idea is to refocus their attention on what is left from what has been lost.

Increase Social Interactions

Social support is another great way to build resilience and grit in children. When kids are surrounded by people who admire them, encourage them and support them through thick and thin, they feel loved and looked after. Social support has been linked to positive emotions, predictability of behavior, and improved self-esteem, motivation, and personal control. Name the ones who always cheer them on when they are faced with difficult emotions. Strong connections with people who love them also make them resilient.

Tell Them It Is Okay to Seek Help

Being brave doesn't always mean dealing with things alone. It also means you can seek assistance when required without feeling ashamed or guilty. After all, two minds are always better than one, so remind them to seek help and not carry all the burdens alone.

Let Them Heal

Often, we presume that resilience is about never failing. But it is about getting back up, recovering, and gaining back control of your life. A lot of times, parents try to rush through an array of emotions, hoping the sooner their system is flushed off them the better. But like any injury, a broken or hurt person needs time to heal. There is a reason why we feel things so deeply. We can't push them away or get over them in a minute. This is deceit and denial, and sooner or later, they will crawl back into our minds and do the damage. The healing time is when one reviews the problem, reflects upon and processes mistakes, and finds means to restore balance. Rushing through emotions doesn't build resilience; embracing and acknowledging them does!

Conclusion

Whenever we are faced with fear, uncertainty, or anxiety and don't respond in a resilient manner, we pass it on to our kids too. As parents, we are always over-directing and overprotecting our kids. We are the sole reason why they turn into risk-averse rule-followers. But these aren't the skills that will help them survive what's out there; their curiosity, adaptability, flexibility, and risk-taking will. This is the mindset that makes them resilient and strong in times of hardships and troubles and allows them to cope with the challenges and failures as they come.

From an early age, we have been rewarding them for memorizing and cramming the right answers. But what we don't realize is their inquisitiveness will be pivotal. Why? Because thanks to technology, they are able to seek answers to god knows whatever comes to their mind with a swipe of their finger in less than 10 seconds. However, once they have the answer, how they use it, process it, evaluate it, and stitch it together is what matters more – again, something that has less to do with cramming and more with how smart and creative they are.

As they grow older and reach their teen years, we force them to compete for trophies, a few slots in a top university, and indirectly preach insensitivity towards others. What we need to teach them instead is collaboration and how they can work flexibly with all types of people in perfect harmony and learn to be responsible for their actions. Tomorrow's world is less about competition and more about collaboration.

What we need to do is teach them to become resilient so that whatever circumstances they have to face, they are mentally and emotionally-prepared to handle them.

In this guide, we hope we have lived up to the promise we started with – to help you prepare your child for the tough and competitive world outside. If we were to do a quick recap of everything that has been covered in this book, it should look something like this – we started off with understanding what resilience means, why our kids need to develop it, and how we can teach them and encourage them using the 7 Cs of building resilience.

In chapter two, we talked about how parents can cultivate and foster creativity in kids and believe and hone their skills and talents to nurture them. We also learned of the importance of discipline and how parents can use empathy to teach rather than use punishment to make them resilient.

In the following chapter, we learned how we can teach children to own up to their mistakes and what role can parents play to correct wrong behavior and approaches using effective strategies.

In chapter four, we saw how we can help kids navigate their way through stress and other negative emotions. We talked about the importance of developing coping skills and presented reader parents with some great ones to get started with.

In the final chapter of the book, we looked at how we can put all the knowledge we have gained into practice. This is, by far, the most crucial step of the entire book. We looked at multiple research studies and tried to understand their links with resilience.

Use this as a guide to better parenting. Identify the things you can work upon and introduce practices that will help your child grow up to become resilient, independent, and ready for the world!

Thank you for giving this book a read. I hope you loved reading it as much as I enjoyed writing it. It would make me the happiest person on earth if you would take a moment to leave an honest review. All you have to do is visit the site where you purchased this book: It's that simple! The review doesn't have to be a full-fledged paragraph; a few words will do. Your few words will help others decide if this is what they should be reading as well. Thank you in advance, and best of luck with your parenting adventures. Every moment is a joyous one with a child.

References

7 C's of resilience. (2017, April 4). Retrieved from
https://activeforlife.com/7-cs-of-resilience/

Ackerman, C. E. (2019, October 4). What is Resilience and Why is It Important to Bounce Back? Retrieved from https://positivepsychology.com/what-is-resilience/

Barker, E. (2014, March 24). How to Raise Happy Kids: 10 Steps Backed by Science. Retrieved from https://time.com/35496/how-to-raise-happy-kids-10-steps-backed-by-science/

Carter, C. (n.d.). 7 Ways to Foster Creativity in Your Kids. Retrieved from https://greatergood.berkeley.edu/article/item/7_ways_to_foster_creativity_in_your_kids

Glembocki, V. (2018). How to Teach Your Kids to Own Their Mistakes. Parents. Retrieved from https://www.parents.com/parenting/better-parenting/advice/teach-kids-to-own-their-mistakes/

Gottfredson, L. S. (1996). What Do We Know About
     Intelligence? i, 15-30.

Hogg, E. (2016, October 24). How to discipline kids:
     Punishment is OUT, Empathy is IN. Retrieved
     from
     https://www.fitmaltamums.com/how-to-
     discipline-kids-punishment-is-out-
     empathy-is-in/

Hyman, S. M., & Sinha, R. (2008). Stress-Related
     Factors in Cannabis Use and Misuse:
     Implications for Prevention and Treatment.
     Journal of Substance Abuse Treatment, 400–413.

Jones, D. E., Greenberg, M., & Crowley, M. (2015).
     Early Social-Emotional Functioning and Public
     Health: The Relationship Between Kindergarten
     Social Competence and Future Wellness.
     American Journal of Public Health, 2283–2290.

Learning from Mistakes: Why We Need to Let Children
     Fail. (n.d.). Retrieved from
     https://www.brighthorizons.com/family-
     resources/the-importance-of-mistakes-
     helping-children-learn-from-failure

Markham, L. (2018, October 11). Don't set your child
     up for extra frustration. Retrieved from
     https://www.mother.ly/child/how-to-
     raise-kids-
     resilience?rebelltitem=11#rebelltitem11

Ong, A. D., Toni, B. L., Wallace, K. A., & Bergeman, C. S. (2006). Psychological resilience, positive emotions, and successful adaptation to stress in later life. *Journal of Personality and Social Psychology*, 730–749.

Oosthuizen, R. M. (2020). Resilience to Emotional Distress in Response to Failure, Error or Mistakes: A Positive Psychology Review. *Springer*, 237-258.

Reznick, C. (2009). The Power of Your Child's Imagination: How to Transform Stress and Anxiety into Joy and Success. New York: TarcherPerigee.

Rubin, K. H., Coplan, R. J., & Bowker, J. C. (2009). Social withdrawal in childhood. *Annual Review of Psychology*, 141-171.

Sharma, M. (2016, July 15). 5 Reasons Why You Should Never Compare Your Kids with Others. Retrieved from https://www.huffingtonpost.in/meha-sharma/five-reasons-why-we-shoul_b_8660618.html

Solomons, K. (2013). *Born to be Worthless: The Hidden Power of Low Self-Esteem.* North Charleston: CreateSpace Independent Publishing Platform.

Waters, L. (2015). The Relationship between Strength-Based Parenting with Children's Stress Levels and Strength-Based Coping Approaches. *Psychology*, 689-699.

What does resilience really mean? (2010, February 20). Retrieved from https://www.diploweb.com/What-does-resilience-really-mean.html

Young, E. (2019, November 5). Five Ways to Boost Resilience in Children. Retrieved from https://digest.bps.org.uk/2019/11/05/five-ways-to-boost-resilience-in-children/

Young, K. (2018, August 30). 20 Powerful Strategies in Building Resilience in Children. Retrieved from https://www.heysigmund.com/building-resilience-children/